RAF Gibraltar

Tony Fairbairn

The Royal Navy ground crew of No.800 Sqdn work on Sea Harrier XZ454 '250' in October 1980. The lettering under the cockpit reads 'Lieutenant Commander TJH Gedge 800 Sqn's CO.' and the code 'N' on the fin indicates HMS *Invincible* from which the Squadron had disembarked.

RAF Gibraltar

TONY FAIRBAIRN

TEMPUS

Tempus Publishing Limited
The Mill, Brimscombe Port,
Stroud, Gloucestershire, GL5 2QG
www.tempus-publishing.com

ISBN 0 7524 2352 5

Typesetting and origination by
Tempus Publishing Limited
Printed in Great Britain by
Midway Colour Print, Wiltshire

Hercules XV201 from RAF Lyneham in the UK leaves Gibraltar on the return leg of another Friday schedule. There is no mistaking one of the 'Pillars of Hercules' in the background!

Contents

Avro Shackleton MR 2, WL751 of Gibraltar-based No.224 Sqdn flies past the southern tip of the Rock. This particular aircraft was originally coded 'B-L' but is shown here wearing the code '3' on its nose for 224's tour of South America in March/April 1957.

Author's Notes

In a book of this format it is possible to provide only a thumbnail sketch of a subject as rich in history as RAF Gibraltar, and so that is exactly what I have set out to do. I have also tried to give due coverage of the airfield's dual role as a civil airport. The photographs are in chronological order, and I have included illustrations of both the airfield site (RAF North Front/RAF Gibraltar) and the harbour site (RAF New Camp). In addition, exercising a little author's licence, I have featured shots of the Saro Windhover which, while not strictly 'RAF Gib', is certainly part of the Rock's colourful aviation heritage. The majority of the later uncreditied photographs I took myself during a three year tour on the Station. Finally, if any readers have interesting photographs taken at RAF Gibraltar I should be delighted to hear from them with a view to perhaps producing a fuller history of aviation on the Rock.

Acknowledgements

I would like to offer my sincere thanks to the following individuals for their help in providing and detailing some of the photographs in this book: Colin Cummings (and his excellent series of books on RAF aircraft accidents); Willie Bell; Jarrod Cotter of *Flypast* magazine; Phil Davies; Peter Elliott at the RAF Museum; Peter Green; Gp-Capt.Mike Hobson; Harry Holmes; David Legg of the Catalina Society; Sean McCourt – a fellow ex-Gibraltar hand; Slim Simpson; David Snow; John Streeter; Andy Thomas; Wing Commander David Trembaczowski-Ryder;

Tony Fairbairn
Chippenham
February 2002

Introduction

Even the most seasoned traveller could not fail to be impressed by that first-time, ground-level view of the Rock of Gibraltar – 1,300ft of sheer limestone towering majestically over the airfield's asphalt acres. The impassive grey cliff face is indented with a handful of viewing galleries from some of the thirty-plus miles of tunnels which honeycomb the Rock, and the view from the top is unforgettably panoramic. As if this unique hallmark was not enough, RAF Gibraltar has a number of other interesting features to concentrate the minds of visiting pilots and air traffic staff alike. Not only does the western end of the runway extend 2,000ft out into Algeciras Bay, but it is also bisected by the main road leading to the Spanish border. Finally, there is the vicious air turbulence generated by the local cool, greasy wind, known as the 'Levanter', which blows over and round the Rock at certain times of the year. In the midst of these unusual characteristics is Gibraltar's key position at the entrance to the Mediterranean, which has resulted in a pronounced, but not exclusive, maritime flavour to military air activity here, in addition to a parallel role as a civilian airport.

The airfield you see today is built on what used to be Gibraltar racecourse and it was from the original equestrian venue that the first aircraft took to the air in 1915. The machines in question were seven landplanes comprising three Caudrons plus four BE 2cs (together with a Short seaplane and two Curtiss H4 flying boats for operations from the harbour). The Royal Naval Air Service had them shipped to Gibraltar for submarine spotting after the first German U-boat had slipped through the Straits into the Mediterranean in May of that year. The technical problems of maintaining this diverse and frail fleet, combined with the unforgiving turbulence, made these early efforts fairly perilous – but at least a start had been made.

It was the U-boat threat which led to plans for the formation of the first RAF squadron, No.265 in August 1918 from Nos 265, 266 and 364 Flights, RNAS. The new unit's equipment was to consist of Felixstowe F.3 and Short 184s for anti-submarine patrols in the Straits. No.265's life was short-lived for it disbanded in 1919.

The inter-war years were quiet and flying was confined to flying boat operations. The Abyssinian crisis brought 210 Sqdn here with its Rangoons and Singapores in September 1935 for what proved to be a twelve-month stay before the unit returned to Pembroke Dock in the UK. In February 1939 four Saro London flying boats of 202 Sqdn, based at Kalafrana, Malta, visited to look at the possibility of using Gibraltar as a permanent base should war break out. A week after hostilities began, the move became permanent and 202 started convoy and anti-submarine patrols, together with sorties to seek out enemy shipping in neutral ports. In order to provide the Army with realistic training in searchlight and sound location techniques, No.3 Anti-Aircraft Co-operation Unit, then based at Kalafrana, Malta, began detachments usually consisting of two Swordfish aircraft.

During 1940, 202 Sqdn patrolled the Straits of Gibraltar and for short-range work took on strength Swordfish floatplanes. Ironically, while 202's Swordfish operated from the harbour, the RN's 810 Sqdn disembarked HMS *Ark Royal* in April with its land-based version of the venerable biplane to start a detachment which would last until May 1941. In order to assist 202 Sqdn with its western Mediterranean patrols, 228 Sqdn based in Egypt sent in detachments of Sunderland flying boats.

The tempo of maritime air activity began to increase in 1941; 202 Sqdn beginning conversion to the vastly superior Catalina in May of that year. The Catalinas were soon in the thick of things, carrying out valuable anti-submarine work in concert with RN ships. By now Gibraltar was firmly established in its role as a stepping stone to more distant bases and, for example, while *en route* to West Africa No.200 Sqdn's Hudsons escorted a batch of forty-eight Hurricanes to Malta. Similarly, in the course of its move to Bathurst, No.204 Sqdn paused here and took the opportunity to fly convoy patrols. More Hudsons, this time in the shape of a detachment from 233 Sqdn in the UK, first appeared in August. By 1942, 233 was mounting the majority of its operations from the Rock and in June of that year Gibraltar became the unit's headquarters. The last quarter of 1941, however, saw considerable RN activity, beginning with the formation, in October, of 779 Sqdn – a Fleet Requirements Unit. Equipped initially with Blackburn Skuas for drogue-towing and coastal defence duties, 779 later acquired Swordfish, Fulmars and Sea Hurricanes, and in April 1943 Defiants replaced the Skuas in the target-towing role. Merlin-engined Beaufighter IIs and Martinets were taken on strength before the FRU disbanded (in August 1945). In November 1941, 700 (Gib) Sqdn was formed here for daily patrols with Walrus flying boats. During the same month the surviving Swordfish of 812 Sqdn found a haven at Gibraltar after the unit's parent ship, HMS *Ark Royal*, had been torpedoed. Regrouping on the Rock, No.812 received new Swordfish which were equipped with radar, and this was used to good effect on 21 December in the first night-sinking of a U-boat (U-451).

But it was in 1942 that RAF Gibraltar sprang to prominence and air activity reached an all-time high, for that year saw Operation TORCH – the allied invasion of North Africa, in which the Station would play a leading part. In preparation for this, Royal Engineers transformed the existing landing strip into a fully tarmacked runway 1,400 yards long – with the last 400 yards protruding into the sea – and 100 yards wide, while dispersal areas were increased to provide parking for up to 600 aircraft. Preparations for TORCH also brought an increase in the flying rate, beginning in February with detachments of 95 Sqdn's Sunderlands from Freetown for convoy escort work. In April No.24 Sqdn started regular communications flights from Hendon using Hudsons, followed in September by a detachment of Whitleys from 161 (Special Duties) Sqdn at Tempsford for clandestine work in North Africa. To control this feverish activity, Air Headquarters Gibraltar was formed, on 1 May, to administer the airfield (RAF North Front) and flying boat activities from the harbour area (RAF New Camp).

With time to the invasion ticking away, shorter range fighter aircraft were shipped from the UK to Gibraltar in crates for assembly on the airfield and for this task a special erection party was established. The mood of urgency gave the work an added impetus and in one nine-day period 122 Spitfires and Hurricanes were assembled.

In the meantime, the Gibraltar-based squadrons had been hard at work hunting submarines and escorting convoys. A large detachment of Catalinas from 210 Sqdn arrived in October to augment the resident 202 Sqdn for the protection of invasion convoys, and on the 24th of the month a 202 Sqdn aircraft picked up Brigadier General Mark Clark (deputy to General Eisenhower, who was to command TORCH) from a submarine following his undercover meeting with resistance leaders in Algiers. The vital job of intelligence gathering for Op TORCH was undertaken by a detachments of 540 Sqdn Mosquitos and 544 Sqdn Spitfires sent out from the UK, and while in Gib the visitors also flew bomb-damage assessment sorties over

Italy. Two Hudson squadrons, Nos 500 and 608, were taken on strength for convoy cover duties, and 179 Sqdn flew in its Leigh Light-equipped Wellington VIIIs for anti-submarine work. In addition, No.511 Sqdn, based at Lyneham in the UK, mounted a Liberator detachment to fly a shuttle service to Malta. With only days to go before TORCH, General Eisenhower himself arrived on 5 November in a B-17 Flying Fortress flown by Major Paul Tibbets, an exceptional pilot who would later become a household name for his role in the atomic bomb raids on Japan in the Superfortress *Enola Gay*.

The assault phase of Op TORCH kicked off promptly at 0100 on 8 November, a day of frantic activity on the airfield. First unit to take off was No.43 Sqdn which had arrived at Gib by sea from the UK a few days earlier. No.43's 18 Hurricanes left before dawn and headed off for Maison Blanche airfield near Algiers, some 300 miles away. The 'Fighting Cocks' were quickly followed by Nos 81 and 242 Sqdns with Spitfires, while later that week Nos 72, 93, 11 and 152 Sqdns (all Spitfires), together with 225 Sqdn (Hurricanes), 255 Sqdn (Beaufighters), and the US Spitfire-equipped 31st and 52nd Fighter Gps all joined the flood of traffic heading out of Gibraltar for North Africa. The resident 233 Sqdn flew 229 anti-submarine sorties in November, during the course of which nine U-boat attacks were made and the squadron lost six aircraft.

Although a peak in air movements was reached in November 1942, the brisk rate of operations continued for the rest of the year. No.179 Sqdn added daylight ops to its Leigh Light night sorties and in December made fourteen U-boat attacks for the loss of four aircraft and three crews. In the same month, No.48 Sqdn arrived with its Hudsons for convoy escort work and by June 1943 was carrying out rocket attacks on enemy subs and shipping. In January 1943, No.248 Sqdn, newly-formed at Predannack in Cornwall with Beaufighters, sent out a detachment to combat Focke Wulf Condors which, from their Bordeaux base, were harassing North Africa-bound allied shipping. The 'Beaus' succeeded in destroying one Condor and damaging another in July.

While Gibraltar had written itself into the history books for its 1942 TORCH effort, 1943 was witness to another equally well-remembered incident, the death of the Polish Prime Minister, General Sikorski, in a Liberator. The 511 Sqdn Liberator, flown by Flight Lieutenant Edward Prchal, left Gibraltar on the night of 4 July carrying the General, his daughter, and members of his personal staff. Shortly after take-off, observers saw the lights of the aircraft begin to descend and moments later it crashed into the sea off the eastern end of the runway. The only survivor was the pilot, Prchal, who, at the subsequent enquiry, stated that the Liberator's controls had jammed. Despite ongoing debate and the advancement of various conspiracy theories, no conclusive explanation of the tragedy has ever really been reached.

Back at the beginning of November 1942 the requirements of TORCH had led to the formation of No.1403 Flight (from the Gibraltar Met Flight) for weather reconnaissance sorties using Gladiators. Now, in September 1943 the Flight was expanded into a full squadron (No.520), which also took over some of 233 Sqdn's Hudsons. Weather flights would now become an important part of RAF Gibraltar's work for a number of years.

During the first half of 1944 several of Gibraltar's squadrons which had been based here to support TORCH departed as the war moved on, the long-serving 202 Sqdn, for example, returning to the UK to train for Leigh Light operations. The dwindling U-boat threat was met by detachments of Liberators from US Navy squadrons VB-112 and VB-114. The year also saw another peak in air activity when the airfield was crowded with Dakotas and other types engaged in Operation DRAGOON – the Allied invasion of Southern France, mounted in August. Another Leigh Light unit to serve on the Rock was the Australian No.458 Sqdn which flew in its Wellington XIVs in January 1945. But with targets becoming ever more scarce, the unit was disbanded in June.

Post Second World War Gibraltar settled into a steady routine as a Coastal Command station, with the accent on visiting aircraft involved in both maritime and navigational exercises. With the disbandment of 520 Sqdn (which had operated Halifaxes, together with

Warwicks for air-sea rescue work) in April 1946, the task of meteorological reconnaissance flights was taken over by a series of detachments from the UK (provided by 518 and 202 Sqdns). This somewhat messy arrangement was regularised, in August 1951, by posting in No.224 Sqdn with Halifaxes as the resident maritime unit, its task comprising both weather flights and general reconnaissance of shipping in the area, particularly that passing through the Straits. A major feature of the 1950s was the busy annual programme of Royal Auxiliary Sqdn 'summer camps'; July 1955, for example, brought in Nos 603 and 614 with Vampires, together with the Meteors of 501 Sqdn. Shackletons replaced the ageing Halifaxes on 224 Sqdn (the last unit to fly them operationally) and these remained on strength until disbandment in October 1966. In that year the Station's name changed from 'North Front' to 'Gibraltar'.

Apart from frequent maritime exercises, both national and NATO, Gibraltar has experienced the occasional change in routine. For example, from mid-1966 until 1978 the base hosted permanent detachments of Hawker Hunter fighters, from UK units (such as, No.229 Operational Conversion Unit), whose role was that of 'guard ship'. Later on, in 1982, up to twelve Hercules per day transited through in support of the South Atlantic conflict.

The Civil Scene

In contrast to the peaks and troughs of military activity, civilian flying tends to be less hectic and more even-paced. Pride of place in the annals of Gibraltar as a civil airport must go to the local airline, Gibraltar Airways. After short-lived operations in 1931 with a Saunders Roe Windhover flying boat from the harbour, the company resumed its activities in 1947, in close co-operation with British European Airways, the latter flying the UK-Gibraltar route and Gib Air servicing Morocco and Spain. Initially Dragon Rapides formed the local equipment, but these gave way, in 1953, to a Dakota – the original 'Yogi Bair' (Yo-Gibair!). This, in turn, was replaced by a Viscount (which immediately took over the 'Yogibair' mantel) for the regular hop across the Straits to Tangier and for the occasional charter flight to such destinations as Lisbon, Casablanca and Lourdes.

Over the years tourism has grown to account for the majority of the commercial traffic, clearly with the accent on the summer months, and this has attracted a wide range of charter operators, in addition to regular schedules by British Airways. The presence of a large British garrison on the Rock has meant a brisk business in air trooping and this has long been contracted out to 'independents' like Dan Air and Britannia.

In addition to 'regular' charter operations there is a steady flow of ad hoc visitors engaged on a multitude of tasks ranging from the rotation of ships' crews to 'one off' freight jobs. Work in this area is often performed by interesting vintage multi-engined aircraft, both jet and piston! Finally, an endless stream of executive, corporate and private types, from Gulfstreams and Learjets to Cessnas, call in on their way to and from Africa and the eastern Mediterranean.

With its very apt motto 'Guard the Gateway' and appropriate badge consisting of a Fortress Key superimposed on sea waves, RAF Gibraltar has played a pivotal role in some epoch-making events down the years. From time to time the Station is required to start engines and answer the call, and the response has always been as solid as the Rock overlooking it.

One
1930-1959

In 1931 this Saunders Roe A.21 Windhover flying boat, G-ABJP was bought for £3,000 to enable the newly-formed Gibraltar Airways to begin experimental services to Tangier in Morocco on 23 September. Other destinations such as Granada and Seville would be covered by special arrangement. The aircraft is seen here in Gibraltar Harbour with La Linea in the background. In the event, operations ceased on 3 January 1932 after 117 return flights due to disappointing utilisation.

In July 1932 the Windhover, by now christened *General Godley* after the then Governor of Gibraltar, was acquired by the Hon. Mrs Victor Bruce, a celebrated figure of her day for her motoring and flying activities. Her plan was to use the amphibian for an attempt on the world flight-refuelled endurance record. She is seen here in Gibraltar before setting off back for England.

A week after the outbreak of the Second World War, No.202 Sqdn, equipped with Saro London flying boats, moved to Gibraltar from Malta, to begin convoy patrols, anti-submarine searches and sorties to locate enemy shipping in neutral ports. This is London II K6932 'TQ:B' of 202 Sqdn, fitted with a long-range saddle tank and carrying four anti-submarine bombs, moored in the harbour.

One of 202 Sqdn's Londons about to be craned onto the shore in order to undergo maintenance in the Spring of 1940. (*H.J. Garlick via Andy Thomas*).

Fairey Swordfish, K8354, 'E-B', of No.3 Anti-Aircraft Co-operation Unit, Spring 1940. Note the 250lb anti-submarine bombs fitted under the wings. (*Via Andy Thomas*).

Early in 1941, No.202 Sqdn re-equipped with Consolidated Catalinas. With their greater range, longer patrols could be flown, and this resulted in an immediate increase in activity. In June of that year, three U-boats were attacked, one being subsequently destroyed by an RN destroyer which a Catalina directed to the scene. This view shows Catalina I AJ159 'AX:B' in the harbour in 1941/1942.

Another Catalina of 202 Sqdn flying over the harbour. This one also bears 202 Sqdn's 'AX' unit code, suggesting that the picture was taken in the period 1941-1943.

From 1942 onwards the Coastal Command colour scheme for Catalinas changed to predominantly white, as displayed by this 202 Sqdn machine on patrol over the Straits of Gibraltar in September 1943.

Catalinas of 202 Sqdn moored in the harbour. In the foreground is FP122 'K', while behind is aircraft 'U'. With the aid of a magnifying glass, some half dozen Hurricanes can be seen lined up on the breakwater, to the left of FP122's rudder. *(The late Ken Jennings via David Legg)*.

This Douglas Boston III AL266 has suffered a collapsed nose wheel. It was probably on a delivery flight to 18 or 114 Sqdn in North Africa some time in 1943. Behind is a Leigh Light Wellington of 179 Sqdn.

A view of the airfield from a Royal Navy Walrus. The parked aircraft all appear to be USAAF B-17 Flying Fortresses. Although US B-17s did not take part in Operation TORCH they did see action once suitable bases were secured in N Africa. Thus this picture was probably taken post-November 1942.

Post-Op TORCH and parking space is at a premium. Here thirty Spitfires and sixteen Hurricanes, distinguishable by the shadows they cast, are parked along the runway jutting out into Algeciras Bay in February 1943. *(J. Streeter)*.

Lockheed Hudson V9168 'V' of 233 Sqdn patrolling over the Straits of Gibraltar in 1943. In October of that year No.233 sent a detachment to the Azores to cover the South Atlantic, but back in Gib the unit continued its anti-submarine work until early 1944. *(Willie Bell)*.

Another Hudson of 233 Sqdn, this one with its bomb doors open, probably carrying out anti-submarine training in Algeciras Bay. The large white vessel in the right hand side of the picture is a hospital ship. *(Willie Bell)*.

No.520 Sqdn was formed at Gibraltar (from 1403 Met Flt) as a meteorological reconnaissance unit in November 1942. Here is the Squadron on parade in October 1945 with one of their Halifax Met IIIs, NA233, in the background. *(Via Andy Thomas)*.

In August 1947 Gibraltar Airways began operating De Havilland 89A Dragon Rapides – initially to Tangier. This particular machine, G-AGEE, was flown by Gibair until 1953. Before taking on a civilian guise, 'EE flew with the Royal Navy as Dominie 1 X7505, and in July 1953 was sold to an Icelandic customer.

In October 1948 224 Sqdn moved to Gibraltar from Aldergrove, Northern Ireland, to become the sole permanent flying unit to be based here. Airborne near the Rock is RG778 'D', one of 224's Halifax GR 6s, which it flew until 1952 when Shackletons took over. The light-coloured disc on the nose of the Halifax is 224's badge: 'On a rock, a tower entwined by a serpent drinking from a lamp therein'. (Peter Green).

De Havilland Hornet F 3 PX340 'W' of 64 Sqdn, Linton-on-Ouse, UK, in 1949. On 15 September 1949 Gp-Capt.A.C. Carver flew another Linton-based Hornet (PX305 'YT-B' of 65 Sqdn) from Bovingdon, UK, to Gibraltar in 3 hours 3 minutes 16 seconds at 357.565mph to set a new Class C1 record. The return flight to the UK on 19 September set another record. Behind the Hornet is an Avro Lincoln.

Echoes of the Second World War – the Catalina is back in Gibraltar. The tall tailfin and radar pod over the cockpit identify this as a Consolidated PBY-6A, serial number 46653 of the US Navy.

Halifax Met VI, RG819, 'B-B', of 224 Sqdn after a mishap in 1952. By now the Halifaxes were becoming worn out and were being replaced by the Shackleton. Note the later colour scheme of black undersides with white top. (*Via Andy Thomas*).

Avro Shackleton MR1 WB856 'B-V' of 224 Sqdn. This particular 'Shack' had a comparatively brief career on the Rock lasting from September 1953 until August 1954 – after which it went to the Joint Anti-Submarine School at Ballykelly, Northern Ireland.

Shackletons of 224 Sqdn. On the left is a Mk 1 (note the blunt tail cone) while on the right is a Mk 2. This dates the shot between May 1953 and August 1954 when 224 operated both marks.

Avro Shackleton MR 2 WL751 'B-L' of 224 Sqdn. No.224 began re-equipping with the Mk 2 in May 1953.

During the 1950s, several airlines used the Avro York for military trooping flights to far-flung corners of the Empire. This York belongs to Air Charter and is G-AMUV *New Venture*. In uniform it served with the RAF as MW226.

Hawker Sea Furies of the Dutch Navy in the early 1950s. Twenty four Sea Fury FB 11s were supplied to the Holland and a further twenty-four were manufactured under licence by Fokker as Sea Fury FB 51s. They served with the Dutch 860 Sqdn and embarked on the aircraft *Karel Doorman*, originally the British Light Fleet Carrier HMS *Venerable*.

Dutch (Kon Marine) Hawker Sea Fury '6-22' taxiing in after landing. The direction of the light on the wet parking area shows the time to be early morning. The shot was taken from an Avro Shackleton, two of whose contra-rotating propellers can be seen at left. RAF Gibraltar's distinctive accommodation blocks can be seen in the background.

Grumman Avenger AS 5, XB314, of the Royal Navy's 815 Sqdn during the period 1953-1955. Note the 'Harp' squadron emblem on the engine cowling. Several Avenger detachments to Gibraltar were mounted during this period. In May 1954 they took part in the anti-submarine Exercise SWITCHBACK and in June participated in an air defence exercise over North West Africa.

North American FJ-3 Fury of the US Navy, in front of a pair of Royal Navy Avengers.

An interesting shot of two RN Fairey Fireflies. Nearest the camera is an AS 6, WD850, while behind is a TT 5 equipped with a target-towing winch under the centreline. The details suggest the aircraft are from 771 Sqdn which operated WD850 until December 1953.

Supermarine Attacker FB 2s of 803 Sqdn, Fleet Air Arm. Nearest is WP300 '151'. The 'J' code on the fin indicates that the machine was embarked on HMS *Eagle*. Behind the Attackers is Avenger XB314 of 815 Sqdn. The shot was probably taken in early 1954.

Shackleton MR 2 WL741 'B-O' of 224 Sqdn on its landing approach over Eastern Beach in 1954. It wears the standard maritime reconnaissance colour scheme of the day which was medium sea grey top surfaces with white undersides. After service with 224 Sqdn '741 went on to earn a crust with 205 Sqdn out in Singapore, and later with 8 Sqdn with whom it was christened 'PC Knapweed'!

Hawker Sea Hawk F 1 WF181 '174'of 806 Sqdn, Fleet Air Arm. No.806's 'Ace of Diamonds' emblem is prominently displayed. The lettering on the nose, just beneath the windscreen appears to read: 'Pilot – Lt T.P. Bourke RN. Pilot's Mate – LA W.F. Wood' The Sea Hawks were probably disembarked from HMS *Eagle* in early 1954.

USAF North American F-86E Sabre 51-13309 lifting off in an easterly direction from Gibraltar's runway. In August 1954 Gibraltar held an exercise to test its air defence capabilities. Taking part were American F-86s. It is possible that the machine shown is from the 357th Fighter Interceptor Sqdn, which was based at Nouasseur Air Base, French Morocco from May 1953 – March 1960.

Douglas Skyraider AEW 1 WT949 '308' of 'A' Flt, 849 Sqdn. The HMS *Eagle* code 'J' is seen on the fin. No.849 Sqdn mounted two detachments to Gib in 1954, the first in March and the second in November, of two aircraft, to carry out trials of a new reflector buoy.

A Lockheed PV-2 Harpoon 'II.S.2' of the French Navy's Escadrille de Servitude IIS. The venerable maritime patrol bomber was here in June 1954 for Exercise SWING.

Sikorsky S-55 coded '8-3' of the Dutch Navy in 1954. The nickname *Cleopatra* is stylishly painted on the nose and the helicopter has probably flown off the Dutch carrier *Karel Doorman*.

Another rare US Navy visitor is this Martin P4M Mercator patrol bomber. Its unusual design featured both piston and jet engines in the nacelles. The aircraft was probably taking part in Exercise SWING.

Douglas R5D-3 Skymaster, Bureau No.92001, of the US Navy's Air Transport Sqdn 24, which was based at Port Lyautey, Morocco. The Sqdn operated three Skymasters.

US Navy Beech SNB-5 Navigator, Bureau No.39289. The legend on the fin states: 'FASRON 104' ie Fleet Air Support Sqdn 104 – its parent unit.

Sikorsky H-19B Chicksaw of the USAF.

This is something of a mystery picture in that it depicts a US Navy Grumman JRF-5 Goose around – apparently – 1954 (with what appears to be a Shackleton in the background). The Goose was a Second World War design and the US Navy phased out the type at the end of that conflict. And yet here is a US Navy Goose, in immaculate condition, attracting interested spectators in the 1950s. It is perhaps a one-off remnant performing an 'Admiral's Barge' role.

Handley Page Hastings of RAF Transport Command. The numbers suggest they are part of the airlift back to the UK of passengers from the troopship *Empire Windrush* which caught fire off Algiers in March 1954.

Far from home is this Swedish-registered Lockheed 18 SE-BTI of Aero Nord. Completing the contemporary scene is the British European Airways Vickers Viking in the background.

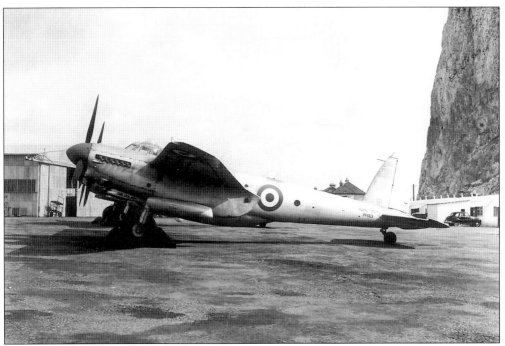

Mosquito PR34 PF663, with PF664 behind, from the RN's 751 Sqdn. The Sqdn was a Radio Warfare Unit within the RAF's Central Signals Establishment at RAF Watton, England. No.751 undertook trials in electronic countermeasures and assisted with Fleet training.

Avro Lancaster ASR/GR IIIs of the School of Maritime Reconnaissance (St Mawgan, UK). Left is SW366 'H-Z', while at right is SW367. The School was the last unit in the RAF to fly the Lancaster operationally. In September 1956 the School was disbanded to form (in conjunction with Coastal Command's 226 Operational Conversion Unit) the Maritime Operational Training Unit (MOTU).

Westland Dragonfly HR 3 WG750 '901'. The code 'J' and fleet number indicates it was from HMS *Eagle* during the period 1953-1955.

French Navy Sud-Ouest SO-94 Corse 1. The type was a crew trainer and communications aircraft, and its name no doubt translates as 'Corsica', rather than 'corse' with a small 'c' which translates as 'full-bodied'!

Lockheed P2V-4 Neptune 'EB/1' of the US Navy. Compare this with the Dutch Neptunes that would still be growling around the Rock in the early 1980s and note here (probably 1954) the solid nose with cannon ports, and the slim tip tanks/searchlight.

Lockheed P2V-5 Neptune 'HB/7' of the US Navy. This version differs from the earlier P2V-4 in having much bulkier tip tanks and a wing-tip searchlight (out of sight on the starboard wing) mounted centrally rather than under-slung, together with a glazed nose. The shot was probably taken c.1954.

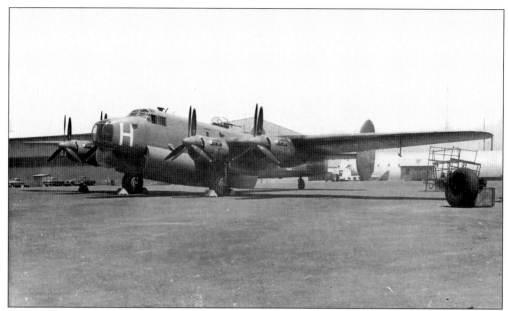

This Avro Shackleton MR 1A, WB855 'C-H' of 236 Operational Conversion Unit was visiting from Kinloss in early 1956. It sports the smart new overall dark sea grey colour scheme, suggested by the OCU as being easier to keep clean, and authorised for the Shackleton force in 1955. Note the old-style white nose code.

Westland Dragonfly HR 3 WG718 '999' from HMS *Ark Royal* in the period 1955-1956. Behind are two other Fleet Air Arm types – Firefly (left) and a Sea Vampire (right).

An interesting feature on this de Havilland Vampire FB 9 is the wing commander's pennant under the cockpit canopy. The serial number, WR239, identifies the aircraft as being operated by the Malta Communications Sqdn. The pennant suggests that it was the 'personal' aircraft of the Malta Sector Commander.

Avro Lincoln B 2s of 199 Sqdn from Hemswell, Lincolnshire. This particular unit specialised in electronic counter-measures work. There is a sad postscript to the centre aircraft, WD131. On 26 June 1955 it was flying at 17,000ft at night over Germany, engaged in a counter-measures exercise, when it was struck by a USAF Sabre of the 496th Fighter Interceptor Sqdn. The Lincoln's starboard wing failed and it crashed killing Flying Officer Hugh Honour and his crew. This picture was taken shortly before the accident.

De Havilland Sea Vampire F 20 VV138 with the code 'FD' of its home at Ford, UK, on the tail. The fighter is from 771 Sqdn – the Southern Fleet Requirements Unit – and is probably part of a 771 Sqdn detachment sent to Gibraltar in June 1955 to assist with the work-up of the aircraft carrier HMS *Ark Royal*.

In 1955 it was the turn of No.614, the only Welsh Auxiliary Sqdn, based at Llandow, to take its Vampire FB 5s out to Gibraltar for its Summer Camp. The two-week detachment lasted from 30 July to 13 August. Here its aircraft are being refuelled prior to another sortie. Note the various types of hot weather uniform. (*P. Davies*).

Two Vampire FB 5s of 614 Sqdn, Royal Auxiliary Air Force, flying south along the eastern side of the Rock. The light patch under the lead aircraft is the water catchment area. Algeciras Bay is above the jets, and beyond that Spain itself. *(P. Davies)*.

A mixed formation of eight Vampire FB 5s of 614 Sqdn, plus three Meteor F 8s, during 614's August 1955 Summer Camp. The squadron markings on the Meteors look very much like No.66's. *(P. Davies)*.

A Vampire T 11 of 614 Sqdn is the nearest type in this August 1955 flight-line. The nose of a camouflaged Vampire FB 5 sticks out, behind which is another silver T 11. Interestingly this bears the unit code 'UU' – that of 226 Operational Conversion Unit. In all probability this aircraft belongs to 614 Sqdn and the code is simply a lingering inheritance. Right at the back is Shackleton MR 2, 'P' of the resident 224 Sqdn. Across the other side of the runway can be seen more of 224's Shackletons. *(P. Davies)*.

Gibraltar, taken from the air in August 1955, with the runway a distinctive feature. On the original print, eight Shackletons can be counted parked on the airfield. (*P. Davies*).

A detachment of Avro Shackletons of 204 Sqdn provided an escort for the BOAC Argonaut *Ajax* flying HRH the Duke of Edinburgh between Gibraltar and Kano in March 1956. The Duke was on his way to Melbourne to open the Olympic Games. HRH is seen emerging from one of the Shackletons in Gibraltar.

HRH the Duke of Edinburgh visiting the RAF's 1152 Marine Craft Unit in Gibraltar harbour in March 1956.

With its cockpit well protected against the elements, this Hawker Sea Hawk FGA 6 XE457 '487' has flown in off HMS *Eagle* with the rest of 899 Sqdn, probably in the first half of 1956.

One of Gibraltar's rarer and more exotic visitors was this North American AJ Savage of the US Navy. A high-performance, carrier-based nuclear strike aircraft, it was unusual in that it was powered by two Pratt & Whitney piston engines (clearly visible!) plus an Allison turbo-jet in the tail (not so obvious). It was not always popular aboard carriers because of its sheer bulk!

Three months after Squadron Leader Mike Hobson took over command of No.603 (City of Edinburgh) Sqdn with its Vampire 5s based at Turnhouse, Scotland, the Auxiliary Air Force unit flew out to Gibraltar for its annual Armament Practice Camp. This is the scene (in July 1956) with WA434, Mike Hobson's normal aircraft, in the foreground. (*Gp-Capt. Mike Hobson*).

Two

1960-Present

The gracefully distinctive lines of de Havilland Comet C 4 XR396 of 216 Sqdn based at Lyneham, UK. VIP work was 216 Sqdn's speciality and '396 probably brought some visiting dignitary to the Rock in the 1960s.

Avro Shackleton MR 3s of the Kinloss Wing, post 1966 when the squadron numbers were no longer applied to the fuselage side. The line-up, from left to right, is as follows: WR975 'A'; XF700 'M'; WR983 'E' and WR990 'N'.

The 'Boscombe Brit'. Bristol Britannia XX367 of the Aeroplane and Armament Experimental Establishment, Boscombe Down, UK. '367's role was the carriage of passengers and freight for overseas trials in the late 1970s and early 1980s, and she is shown doing just that in Gibraltar.

McDonnell Douglas Phantom FG 1 XV590 '004' of the RN's 892 Sqdn. The photograph was probably taken during one of 892 Sqdn's embarkations on HMS *Ark Royal* during the 1970s.

Blackburn Buccaneer S 2 of 809 Sqdn disembarked from HMS *Ark Royal* in the 1970s, alongside one of 892 Sqdn's Phantoms. The Buccaneer is equipped with an air-to-air refuelling pod under its starboard wing.

Nearest the camera is PBY-6A Catalina C-FHNF, with a second Cat behind which is probably C-FHNH. Both machines are in the markings of the French Protection Civile based at Marseille, and they are probably on their way back to their new operators, Avalon Aviation in Canada, in 1974, after their Gallic service which began ten years earlier. Colour scheme is natural metal with red nose, cowling trim and wing tips, and black arrow-head on the tail. The French *tricolore* can just be discerned at the top of the tailfin. (*J. Streeter*).

Two classic RAF types from the early 1970s. Nearest is Argosy XP439 of 115 Sqdn, out from its base at Cottesmore, UK to check Gibraltar's airfield aids, while behind is Britannia XL496, normally based at Brize Norton. (*J. Streeter*)

For a long time through the 1970s a detachment of Hawker Hunters was maintained at Gibraltar as guard aircraft, and for example, in August 1973, No.229 Operational Conversion Unit based at Chivenor, Devon sent out three aircraft to cover the commitment. Pictured from that detachment is Hunter FGA 9, XF445 'Q' wearing the markings of No 79 'Shadow' Sqdn. The RAF fighter is formating with a North American RA-5C Vigilante reconnaissance aircraft from the US carrier *Independence* over the Straits of Gibraltar. (*J. Streeter*).

The Merchantman was a freight conversion of the Vickers Vanguard airliner. Here, Merchantman G-APES of Air Bridge Carriers unloads freight on the night of 7 February 1980.

Saturday 16 February 1980 and this Canberra PR 7 WT532 of 13 Sqdn is well protected against the uncertain Mediterranean weather over the weekend. The crew will no doubt be looking for bargains in Main Street and on the coming Monday will fly back to their home base of Wyton in the UK.

Grumman C-2A Greyhound 155123 'JM/34' from US Navy Sqdn VR-24 in February 1980. The Greyhound's role is carrier on-board delivery, as signified by the letters COD on the engine nacelle and this particular aircraft was based at Sigonella, Sicily. The pilots names, 'Lt James; Lt J.G. Brewer', are stencilled under the windscreen.

Amongst the aircraft arriving on 21 February 1980 was this Canberra T 17 WJ565 'C' of 360 Sqdn, Wyton. More interestingly, its pilot was Lt-Com. Peter Sheppard who, in his spare time, delighted air show spectators with his displays in the RN Historic Flight's Sea Fury.

Even the best regulated airlines must respond to the seasonal vagaries of air travel and on 23 February 1980 this Dutch-registered Boeing 737-2K2 of Transavia called in to Gibraltar on lease to British Airways.

Breguet Atlantic '250' of the Dutch Navy's 321 Sqdn on 24 February 1980. The Atlantics were regular visitors to Gibraltar participating in NATO exercises.

Lockheed C-130F Hercules 149797 'JM' from the US Navy's VR-24 Sqdn detachment at Rota, Spain. The shot was taken on 6 March 1980 and the 'Herc' was on a routine freight run.

Another detachment from the Fleet Requirements and Air Direction Unit in the shape of Canberra TT 18 WE122 '845'. The Canberra was providing target-towing facilities for RN units operating around Gibraltar. To the left of the picture is the tail of one of the Unit's Hunter GA 11s.

Like the Royal Navy's FRADU, the RAF also operated the Canberra TT 18 in the target facilities role. No.7 Sqdn at St Mawgan in Cornwall was the unit concerned whose WK124 (shown) arrived in Gibraltar on 27 February 1980 in company with the Squadron's T 4.

The seven stars of the constellation Ursa Major appropriately form No.7 Sqdn's badge, part which is prominently displayed on this Canberra WJ879. The solid nose helps identify it as a T 4 trainer.

Nimrod XV257 from the Kinloss Wing, visiting on 2 March 1980 for one of the countless maritime exercises held in the Mediterranean.

Exercise SPRING TRAIN had drawn an impressive number of RN ships to Gibraltar when C-in-C Fleet, Vice-Admiral Sir James Eberle, called in on HS 125, XX508 on 24 March 1980.

Luton-based Cessna Titan II, G-BELV, owned by Irvine Sellars, was on its way to Biarritz when it dropped in on 15 March 1980.

In addition to endless exercises, Gibraltar was the scene of periodic trials work. Flight Refuelling's Tarrant Rushton-based Canberra TT 18, WK143 was in Gibraltar in mid-March 1980 for low-level target-towing trials with the frigate HMS *Broadsword*.

Westland Lynx HAS 2 XZ256 '466/AT' from the Leander Class frigate HMS *Argonaut* – 14 March 1980.

The sun doesn't always shine in Gibraltar! BAC 1-11 XX919 from the Royal Aircraft Establishment, Bedford – a support aircraft for a detachment of RAE Gnat aircraft taking part in Exercise SPRING TRAIN. 18 March 1980.

Westland Sea King HAS 2 XV698 '581' of 'B' Flt 824 Sqdn, disembarked from the Royal Fleet Auxiliary *Fort Austin*. 24 March 1980.

The UK Civil Aviation Authority's HS 125 Srs 3B G-AVDX on 24 March 1980.

Swiss-registered Learjet HB-VCW which flew in from Rabat on 8 March 1980 was typical of the more exotic corporate business aircraft to pay fleeting visits to Gibraltar.

Sunday 30 March 1980 and Exercise SPRING TRAIN flying came to an end. This FRADU Hunter XE689 '864' is coming in to land over Eastern Beach after one of the final sorties of the exercise.

Saturday 29 March 1980 – but the show goes on despite the weekend! Canberra T 22 WT510 '854' from the Fleet Requirements and Air Direction Unit after a late SPRING TRAIN sortie.

Visitors from Decimomanu were a regular feature of the weekend aviation picture, and on 29 March 1980 the slot was filled by two Harrier GR 3s from 3 Sqdn. Centre is XZ134 'J' (Wing Commander G.R. Profit AFC) while just visible on the right is the proboscis of XV808 'W' (Fl. Lt S.J. Underwood). At left is one of FRADU's ubiquitous Hunters.

An interesting feature of the several Vickers Merchantmen operated by the cargo line Air Bridge Carriers was the different colours schemes sported by the aircraft. Unloading freight in late March 1980 is G-APEG.

Westland Wasp HAS 1 XT784 '432' from the *Leander* Class frigate HMS *Scylla*. Behind are Wasp XT779 '322' and Wessex HU 5 XS522 '347' from the RN ships *Active* and *Kent* respectively. 31 March 1980.

Pilot Shaun Clements checks on the turnround of Gnats XP513 (front) and XP505 from the Royal Aircraft Establishment, Farnborough, at the end of Exercise SPRING TRAIN – 26 March 1980.

The package tour industry brought all manner of airliners to the Rock including, on 21 April 1980, Dan Air BAC 1-11, G-ATPL. The aircraft was on charter to the holiday company Marshall-Sutton.

British Airways Trident II G-AVFE turning round at Gibraltar on 1 April 1980 during the first flight of the summer schedule for that year. The Trident was not ideally suited to the UK-Gibraltar run and on this occasion 'VFE had to de-fuel and then fly on to Tangier to refuel again.

Convair VC-131F, 141020 was the personal aircraft of the C-in-C Allied Forces Southern Europe and flew in from Sigonella, Sicily on 14 April 1980. Powered by piston-engines, it was one of the few larger aircraft to require aviation gasoline – Avgas (as opposed to jet fuel). Because of its high profile VIP role it became a factor to be reckoned with in plans to dispose of large stocks of Avgas occupying tankage in RAF Gibraltar's underground William's Way fuel depot.

Like the other US Navy types from VR-24, this Rockwell CT-39G Sabreliner 159363 'JM/12' plied the Mediterranean routes and was a periodic visitor to Gibraltar from its base at Sigonella, Sicily.

Westland Wessex HU 5 XS522 '347' nicknamed *Buzby*, from HMS *Kent*. *Buzby's* task on the day it was photographed – 8 April 1980 – was nothing more warlike than providing air experience flights for air cadets lucky enough to come to Gibraltar for their Easter Camp.

Vickers Vanguard F-BTOV of French-registered Europe Aero Services was in Gibraltar on 9 April 1980 to pick up a ship's crew and take them back to Marseilles.

This close-up of Sea King HAS 2 XZ577 '582' from the Royal Fleet Auxiliary *Fort Austin* highlights the helicopter's nickname *The Bitch*. What was she doing in Gibraltar on that day? Well, three passengers got off the Britannia Airways 737 G-BGYJ which arrived earlier in the day and climbed straight into the Sea King – to carry out surveillance of a Russian naval exercise which was going on at the time.

Westland Lynx HAS 2 XZ238 '450' disembarked from the frigate HMS *Sirius* in mid-April 1980. The Lynx is carrying an underslung load of stores for its parent vessel.

Brize Norton-based Andover E 1, XS639 of 115 Sqdn on All Fool's Day, before calibrating the airfield Precision Approach Radar.

Andover C 1 XS607 from the Royal Aircraft Establishment, Bedford, photographed on 15 April 1980 while acting as a support aircraft for a detachment of Gnat aircraft from the same unit.

The ranks of VIPs visiting Gibraltar in connection with exercise activity were swelled on 1 April 1980 by the arrival of the NATO commander of Iberian Atlantic Command (COMIBERLANT) in a Portugese Air Force Casa C.212A Aviocar, (serial number 6506). The Spanish-designed STOL utility transport departed the following day.

Conveniently parked on the south side of the airfield, within camera-reach from the author's office window, these Dutch Navy SP-2H Neptunes of 320 Sqdn (Valkenburg) thundered into Gib for Exercise OPEN GATE. Shown, on 28 April, are '201', '202' and '210'.

In 1980 the Cold War still influenced everyday operational flying activity and the RAF packed a powerful punch in Germany, including these Bruggen-based Jaguars of 31 Sqdn. In front is 31's two-stick T 2 trainer XX844 'DZ', on 26 April.

The Royal Netherlands Air Force's 334 Sqdn (at Soesterburg) provided this Fokker F-27 Troopship as a support aircraft for the Kon Marine's Neptunes flying in Exercise OPEN GATE.

A most unusual visitor on 25 April 1980 was this Agusta-Bell AB212 ASW serialled 'M.M.80957' and coded '7-26' which flew in from the Italian frigate *Carabiniere*.

Towards the end of April 1980 the participating aircraft began assembling in Gibraltar for the NATO Exercise OPEN GATE. The West German Navy input included this Atlantic, 61+05 of 1 Staffel, Marinefliegerschwader 3 'Graf Zeppelin', based at Nordholz, Germany.

No.2 Sqdn was a tactical reconnaissance and ground attack outfit based at Laarbruch, Germany when it flew this pair of Jaguars out to Gibraltar in April 1980.

Capital Air Surveys certainly catered for both ends of the market! On the one hand they operated a vintage Beech D18, and on the other this sparkling Learjet 25C, N9HN, seen on 8 May 1980.

A visiting US Navy admiral dropped in on 28 April 1980 courtesy of this Canadian CH-124 12406 from HMCS *Annapolis*.

In addition to the single-seat version of the Hunter, the Fleet Requirements and Air Direction Unit also operated a number of two-seat T 8s, including XF358 '875' shown here on 2 May 1980.

The irrepressible RN sense of humour is once again to the fore on this Wasp XT415 '452', photographed on 7 May 1980. Beneath the words 'Royal Navy' is the contemporary reciprocal arrow logo of British Rail, clearly spawned by the helicopter's parent ship code 'BR' of HMS *Brighton*.

Nimrod R 1, XW664 of 51 Sqdn sits innocuously on the pan wearing its original grey/white maritime paint scheme. The published squadron histories describe 51's role as 'radar reconnaissance', and best we leave it at that.

Cessna 402 Businessliner PJ-SAA, operated by Turbo-System on 7 May 1980.

Detachment aircraft require a spares backup, often formed into a 'flyaway pack', and these, together with any specialist ground equipment, need to be flown to the detachment base. Hohn-based C.160D Transall 50+89 of Lufttransportgeschwader (LT) 63 was operating was operating in just a role in support of Germany's OPEN GATE Atlantic maritime patrol aircraft.

RAF Gibraltar's 1980 Open Day was held on 10 May and amongst the aircraft that flew in for the occasion was this Wessex HU 5 XT450 'V' of 845 Sqdn. At the time helicopter was embarked on the assault ship HMS *Intrepid*.

'Not a bad place for a night stop' thought the crew of this P-3 Orion '153424/S/LE' of the US Navy's VP-11 after it had flown in from Sigonella, Sicily on 9 June 1980.

When Gibraltar Airways' own Viscount went back to Cardiff for periodic overhaul a replacement aircraft was always flown out to maintain the daily schedules to Tangier. In 1980 British Airways plugged the gap with one of their own Viscounts, G-AOYP, pictured here on 23 May.

The eruption of Mount St Helens in Washington state, USA, on 18 May 1980 brought out the Meteorological Research Flight's one-off Hercules W 2, XV208 at short notice from its UK base at Boscombe Down. During its five-day stay the 'Herc', with its crew of RAF and Met Office personnel, was tasked with ascertaining the accuracy of the predicted movement of the residual dust in the atmosphere.

The flurry of naval activity in May 1980 also brought in this Wessex HAS 3 XP150 '406/AN' from the destroyer HMS *Antrim*.

When the flying training schools sent aircraft to Gibraltar they were almost always in groups rather than simply singletons. When Jetstream T 2, XX468 '560' of the RN's 750 Sqdn (pictured) flew out from Culdrose on 10 May 1980 it was accompanied by XX476 '561'.

St Mawgan-based Nimrod XV226 finally departed Gibraltar on 10 July 1980 after a three-day delay due to a bird strike which had caused sufficient damage to warrant an engine change.

French-registered Learjet F-GCMS transiting through on 18 June 1980. The propeller at left is from one of the Rolls Royce Dart engines of Gibair's Viscount.

You certainly couldn't accuse Southern Air Transport of squandering money on a flashy paint scheme for their L-383 Hercules N9266R, which arrived late at night on 17 June 1980. It left the following day carrying pipeline equipment for Marseilles.

Noble Aviations's Piper Navajo G-BGCC pictured on 11 June 1980. Behind sits 'Yogibair', Gibraltar Airways' own Viscount, ready for another short hop across the Straits of Gibraltar to Tangier.

Gutersloh-based No.4 Sqdn flew in their Harrier T 4 trainer XW272 'CZ' (along with a single-seater) on Saturday 2 August 1980. Pilots' names stencilled under the cockpit canopy were Flt Lt J.D. Clark (front) and Sqdn Ldr R.H. Fletcher (rear).

XX119 ('Flt Lt F.L. Turner' stencilled under the cockpit) was one of four Jaguars of 54 Sqdn (Coltishall, UK) that took the opportunity to drop in for a few days in July 1980 during their detachment to Decimomanu, Sardinia.

Nearly the last word in 'biz' jets! Cessna Citation II, appropriately registered G-JETA by its owners, IDS Aviation, and caught as it passed through on 30 July 1980.

With the early morning sun casting shadows on its elegant lines, this Lockheed P-3C Orion arrived from Sigonella, Sicily, on Friday 25 July 1980 for a weekend stay. Serialled '158916/LF' it was on the strength of US Navy squadron VP-16.

Visiting Jaguars also included this T 2 trainer XX146 of 54 Sqdn, Coltishall, UK. The two-seater enabled the squadron engineering officer to escape from 'Deci' and sample the delights of Gibraltar!

Andover XS596 of 115 Sqdn, Brize Norton. Although 115's aircraft normally wore a red/white colour scheme for their calibration duties, '596 is still sporting its tactical transport brown/sand camouflage from a previous life with 46 Sqdn. The pilot was Flt Lt Gerry Marshall, and the date 10 July 1980.

The Nimrod, in the maritime patrol role and colour scheme, is a familiar site in Gibraltar, but this particular machine, XV148 from the Royal Aircraft Establishment, Bedford is noticeably different with its red markings. It arrived for trials work on 30 November 1980 with the call sign 'Black Box'.

In addition to its Sea Harriers, *Invincible* disembarked its Wessex HU 4. Serialled XT486 and coded '437' it bore the Nickname 'Bumble'.

Sea Harriers of 800 Sqdn disembarked from HMS *Invincible* in October 1980. Nearest is XZ454 '250' (the personal aircraft of 800's CO, Lt-Com. Tim Gedge), while behind is XZ460 '253'.

No exercises to speak of were under way when this Dutch Navy (Kon Marine) Neptune was photographed in early November 1980 and in all probability it was having a look at Soviet surface units exercising in the area.

Time spent on reconnaissance is rarely wasted – goes the saying. And that is precisely what this P-3C Orion was doing in August 1980. The mission pictured was in preparation for Exercise DISPLAY DETERMINATION, which would be held the following month. The aircraft shown is '156518/LQ/1' from US Navy squadron VP-56 – 'The Dragons'.

Whilst operating in the area during October 1980, 800 Sqdn's Sea Harriers took the opportunity to have a look at this Mod Kashin guided missile destroyer of the Soviet Navy as it passed through the Straits of Gibraltar. (*MOD Navy*).

Piper Navajo G-BFKJ registered to Air Messenger Ltd on 8 August 1980.

Weekend visiting Harrier T 4 XZ145 'AT' of Gutersloh-based 3 Sqdn, on 1 February 1981. Pilot names under the cockpit were 'Flt Lt Alsford' and 'Sqdn Ldr K.G. Grumbley'. To the left of the 'T-bird' is accompanying Harrier GR 3, XW630 'AG'.

When Wasp XT420 '422' flew in from the frigate HMS *Aurora* in late November 1980 it immediately went unserviceable. Here it is being air-tested on 3 December following maintenance to rectify the snags.

Built in 1951, this Beech D18S CF-DTN of Capital Air Surveys was based at Pembroke, Ontario, and was engaged in survey work in Algeria. A long way from home, it was photographed on 5 December 1980.

Beech UC-12B (Super King Air) 161197 '8D' brought in US Navy personnel on 23 January 1981 to attend a planning meeting.

The wing commander's pennant under the cockpit of this Shackleton AEW 2 WL757 marks it out as the flagship of 8 Sqdn (Lossiemouth, UK). '757 was no stranger to the Rock for from December 1961 to March 1966 it was on the strength of Gibraltar's own Shackleton squadron, No.224, coded 'C'.

Most of the fast jet squadrons using the NATO range at Decimomanu, Sardinia, flew across to Gibraltar for a weekend break and here are four Jaguars (three GR 1s plus a two-seat trainer) of 20 Sqdn doing just that.

One of the tasks of this BAC 1-11, XX105 of the Royal Aircraft Establishment, Farnborough was the airlift of freight to and from trials locations. Although in military harness, its distinctive colour scheme of yellow under-surfaces, red fuselage stripe and white top immediately caught the eye when it arrived for a two-day stay on 9 December 1980.

The crew of this Lockheed C-141A Starlifter, 66-0204 of the 438th Military Airlift Wing probably did some extra careful flight planning before flying into Gibraltar on 29 January 1981. The big transport brought in spares from Norfolk, Virginia for a US Navy submarine in the dockyard. Flight time from Norfolk was 7 hours 30 minutes and after the Starlifter had disgorged its load it took off for Ramstein.

Cessna Citation II, D-IGLU, arrived from Nuremburg on 2 December 1980 for an 'overnighter'.

The Canadians have arrived – and pictured on 4 February is some of their contribution to TEST GATE '81. Framed by a Canadair Argus maritime patrol aircraft is the Canadian support Hercules 130311 of 435 Sqdn from Edmonton.

A brace of Navy Wessex HU 5s. Front is XS513 'V.P' from *Bulwark*, while behind is XT480 '636' off the RFA *Regent*. In the background, over the other side of the runway, are two TEST GATE Argus.

A typically busy scene during TEST GATE, a NATO exercise held in February 1981. Parked Canadian Argus and a US Navy P-3B Orion getting airborne, provide a backdrop for Wessex HU 5 XS513 'V-P' from HMS *Bulwark*.

US Navy P-3B Orion 153414 '85' of VP-8 (from Rota, Spain) framed by the Magnetic Anomaly Detection (MAD) tail-cone of a Canadian Armed Forces Argus during Exercise TEST GATE in February 1981.

Canadair Argus 10741 (nearest) and 10733 of VP-415 (Summerside) are prepared for another sortie during Exercise TEST GATE.

You can almost hear the roar of Argus 10741's four massive Wright turbo-compound piston engines as it thunders majestically past the Rock at the end of another TEST GATE sortie.

Wessex HAS 3 XM837 '407' pictured on 10 February 1981. The helicopter had flown in off
HMS *Bulwark*.

British Leyland chartered this Lockheed L-100 Hercules to airlift a corporate display to Gibraltar.
Operated by Transamerica its registration is N11ST, and wearing its attractive white/green/silver
the Herc is tucked away on the south side of the airfield on 7 March 1981.

Different aeroplanes – same engines. Mid-March and RAF Hercules C 3 XV177 provides airflow for US Navy P-3C of VX-1 which had an unserviceable port outer engine. In other words – a 'buddy-buddy' start. This is an interesting picture in that XV177 was the first RAF stretched 'Herc' to visit Gibraltar, touching down on 14 March 1981.

Full side view of VX-1's troublesome P-3. The aircraft in question has serial number 157326 and is coded '5/JA'.

In addition to the P-3, US Navy squadron VX-1 fielded a Lockheed S-3A Viking, '160592/17/JA', both aircraft coming from Patuxent River. The carrier-borne anti-submarine twin-jet is pictured on 17 March 1981.

A one-off task brought in this British Caledonian BAC 1-11, G-ASJC *City of Glasgow* on 18 March 1981.

A couple of hours drive from Gibraltar, up the east coast of Spain, is the attractive port of Marbella – something of magnet for the rich and the famous, where can be seen some quite awesome private yachts. The more lavish pack a small helicopter in which to nip ashore in style. This Hughes 500, N779FA, pictured in Gibraltar on 20 March 1981, was one such 'tender' and came from the motor yacht *Nonstop*.

Basking in spring sunshine on 24 March is Canberra PR 9, XH165 of Wyton-based 39 Sqdn, on a routine 'navex'. Skulking in the background, 32 Sqdn HS 125, XW789 brought in General Sir Jack Harman the previous day.

98

Canberra E 15, WH972 of Marham-based 100 Sqdn, with engine and hatch covers in place for its three-day stay, photographed on 27 March 1981.

Dassault Falcon 20F, G-BGOP of Datsun (UK) Ltd in March 1981.

Convair 580, LN-BWG of the Norwegian airline Nor-Fly Charter about to take a ship's crew home from Gibraltar on 7 April 1981.

Cessna 340 II, G-BFJS of Northair Aviation on 10 April 1981.

Beech Super King Air F-BXOL, with Gibair's Viscount in the background, 10 April 1981.

Pilot Derek Morter (well known for his work with the *Blue Herons* aerobatic team) starts up Fleet Requirements and Air Direction Unit Hunter GA 11 XE716 '834' prior to another sortie with an RN task group in the waters near Gibraltar. Watching are ground crew Tom Beck and Steve Broughton. The occasion is Exercise SPRING TRAIN and the date is 11 April 1981.

The start of another SPRING TRAIN mission for P-3C Orions 158929 '6/LP' and 158920 '7/LP' of VP-49, detached from their home base of Jacksonville, Florida.

Buccaneer S 2s of 12 Sqdn (Lossiemouth, UK). The nearest two aircraft are XW527 and '537, while in the background are two Nimrods, including XV233 from 42 Sqdn at St Mawgan, all at Gibraltar for the UK national Exercise SPRING TRAIN in April 1981.

Andover CC 2, XS794 of 32 Sqdn, Northolt, on a routine 'navex' to Gibraltar on 27 April 1981.

RAF Gibraltar's station commander, an air commodore in the 1980s, also wore a NATO hat, that of Commander Air Operations Gibraltar (COMAIRGIB). This P-3C '158923/7/LA' of US Navy squadron VP-5, had just brought the air commodore plus Flag Officer Gibraltar back from a NATO conference in Naples.

During 1981-1982 British Airways trialled the operation of a TriStar at Gibraltar. While not cloaked in secrecy the test was certainly undertaken discreetly for some reason. Here the TriStar, G-BBAJ *The Elizabeth Harkness Rose*, lifts off in an easterly direction.

Westland Wasp HAS 1, XT436 '421' from the Leander Class frigate HMS *Galatea* on 5 May 1981. This particular Wasp was nicknamed *Albert* and had pigs painted on its side. The story behind this is that the captain of *Galatea* was also known as 'Captain Pugwash' after the piratical TV cartoon figure whose ship was the *Black Pig*. When *Galatea* was commissioned the captain said: 'I may be Captain Pugwash but this ship is not the *Black Pig!*'

Calgary-based HS 125 Srs 400, C-GCEO of Bailey Aviation, staging through Gibraltar on 21 May 1981.

C-9A Nightingale, 10881 of the USAF's 55th Aeromedical Airlift Sqdn based at Rhein-Main, made a brief visit on 10 July 1981.

Rota (in Spain) is clearly the home base of this US Navy Sikorsky SH-3G '149000' which called in on 16 July 1981.

Beech King Air 90, D-IBUR, after touching down from Offenburg on 31 July 1981.

Nimrod XV250 of 236 OCU, Kinloss on 1 August 1981. This particular aircraft was one of two Nimrods (the other being XV231) providing search and rescue cover for the visit of the Prince and Princess of Wales.

US-registered Swearingen Merlin IIIB, N1013N, which transited through on 6 August 1981.

Boeing 737, N54AF of Air Europe/Air Florida, about to depart for Luton on 17 August 1981. The 737 was on lease to Britannia Airways at the time.

Swiss-registered Bell 212, HB-XKG, parked up on 14 September 1981. The helicopter belonged to a Saudi prince.

Wearing its Danish registration OY-MBB, this Super King Air of Midtfly arrived on 15 September 1981 and departed the following day.

One of the more diminutive types to park under the Rock, this is Beechcraft Bonanza D-EMEG which called in from Germany on 22 September 1981.

'The logical way to fly' proclaims the logo on this Piper Aztec 250, G-BATE, of Air Logistics. The Aztec had flown in from Biggin Hill on 27 September 1981 and seems to be anchored down for a protracted stay.

Rarely seen in Gibraltar, Air UK flew in BAC 1-11, G-AXMU *Island Esprit* on 15 Oct 1981 for a one-off charter.

Boeing 727 G-BIUR of Dan Air takes off on 29 October 1981. This was quite an emotional occasion for the operations and air movements staff on the Station as it was the last flight of Dan Air's Ministry of Defence, twice-weekly, trooping contract to Gibraltar. The keenly-fought contract had been won by Britannia Airways whose Boeing 737s would now become a familiar sight on the Rock.

The air turbulence around Gibraltar is legendry, and this HS 125, XW930, from the Royal Aircraft Establishment, Bedford had come out to Gibraltar in early December 1981 to conduct gust research.

Lockheed P-3C Orion '158570/42/LN' of US Navy squadron VP-45 arrived on 4 January 1982 for a detachment lasting about a week.

Vickers Viscount G-BDRC *Sarnia II* in the colours of Guernsey Airlines in early January 1982.

In 1981 Gibraltar Airways changed its name for commercial reasons to 'GB Airways'. Shown here in 1982 after a January rainstorm is the airline's Viscount G-BBVH.

An echo of earlier times, Dakota G-AMPO of Air Atlantique in early morning sunshine on 23 January 1982.

Vickers Merchantman G-APES in its smart new Air Bridge paint scheme on 17 February 1982. Freight is being loaded using a fork-lift truck after the scissors platform originally trundled up for the job developed an alarming hydraulic leak!

Buccaneer S2B XV863 'U' from 16 Sqdn, Laarbruch, Germany, pictured on 19 February 1982. The day before, this aircraft aborted its take-off due to suspect nose wheel steering and engaged the Chain Arrestor Gear (CHAG). This consists of an arrestor wire attached to heavy anchor chain. The Buccaneer stopped right on the runway threshold, with only metres to go before Eastern Beach and the sea.

Lockheed P-3 Orion '160999/6/LJ' of VP-23 which had flown in for Exercise SPRING TRAIN, due to start on Monday 22 March 1982.

US Navy Douglas C-9B '159117/JU', *City of Norfolk*, from VR-56, being turned round on 28 March 1982.

Vickers Viscount G-AVJB *Jane* of British Air Ferries, in Gibraltar on 18 March to take the crew of the SS *Uganda* back to the UK.

No.17 Sqdn (Bruggen, Germany) decided to send four of their Jaguars to Gibraltar for the weekend and selected XX821 'BF'. XZ381 'BL', XZ371 'BB' and XX768 'BA'. They were photographed from the author's office window on 21 May 1982.

De Havilland Comet 4, XV814, (civil registration G-APDF) operated by the Royal Aircraft Establishment's Radio Flight, on 15 May 1982. The aircraft is wearing RAE's distinctive 'raspberry ripple' colour scheme. Basically, it was a long-range platform for a wide variety of trials work, and its hybrid mixture of Comet nose and Nimrod tail inevitably led to its nickname of 'Conrod'! Its last flight was to Boscombe Down on 29 January 1993, to provide spares for Comet 4, XS235 *Canopus*, and it was finally scrapped in July 1997.

Another exercise scene, this time OPEN GATE in May 1982. Two P-3s provide an international flavour – Canadian CP-140 Aurora 140106 from VP-415 is nearest, while taking off in the background is US Navy Orion '161004/4/LJ' from VP-23.

Boeing 737 OY-MBZ of Maersk Air being turned round on 21 June 1982.

In June 1982 Gibraltar had a 'permanent' detachment of Jaguars, provided by 54 Sqdn. On the twenty-first of the month the Jaguar ranks were swelled by the arrival of No.6 Sqdn's T 2 XX146 'S' (front) and XX727 'GJ' from 54 Sqdn (behind).

Nimrods XV226, '233 and '245 from 42 Sqdn, which had flown in from their base at St Mawgan on 23 July 1982 for Exercise JOLLY ROGER.

US Navy P-3 Orion '152179/4/LY' of VP-92 lifting off the runway on 26 June 1982.

The 'flying classroom' for Fleet Air Arm Observers, this Jetstream T 2, ZA110 '573' of 750 Sqdn was visiting from its base at Culdrose on 4 July 1982.

When this shot was taken in July 1982, Air Europe was a thriving airline operating regular schedules to Gibraltar. The Boeing 737's registration is G-BMEC.

Appropriately registered G-ZEAL, this Learjet 35A was operated by CSE Aviation when it called in on 20 July 1982.

No.6 Sqdn flew in six Jaguars on 23 July for a weekend stopover, (probably from Decimomanu, Sardinia) of which this is XX739 'EE'.

GB Airways' own Viscount 'Yogibair' may have seemed tireless and omnipresent but even it had eventually to return to the UK for a rebuild. When that finally happened British Air Ferries Viscount G-APEY was sent out as a replacement – on 27 September 1982.

Although RAF Jaguars were fairly frequent visitors to Gibraltar, No.41 Sqdn's aircraft were rarely seen. Based at Coltishall, Norfolk, No.41's role is reconnaissance and seen here on 22 October 1982 is one of the unit's Jaguar GR 1s, XZ119 'G'.

Almost falling into the 'vintage' category, these Canadian Armed Forces T-33A Silver Stars had flown in from Salon de Provence via Decimomanu on Friday 22 October for the customary weekend stay. Their serials are 130450 and 130542.

Four Buccaneers from 208 Sqdn, Honington, made a mid-week visit on 10 November 1982. They were XX901, XV161, XN981 and XZ430, and this is one of them. The sign reads: 'Danger – Aircraft Armed'.

Unfortunately, this Rockwell Sabreliner is somewhat anonymous apart from the fact that its registration is N65L. The rather suave black and gold colour scheme suggested a wealthy private owner when it was photographed on 4 December 1982.

G-TALL was the first production Jetstream 31 and is seen here on 14 December while on a demonstration tour of the Mediterranean area. The aircraft had arrived from Rabat, Morocco and was flying on to Malta.

Home by Christmas. Another Nimrod R 1 of 51 Sqdn, this time XW666 in December 1982. The aircraft is wearing the new overall 'hemp' paint scheme.

Previously registered G-ZEST, this Learjet 35 has now been given the even more appropriate G-LEAR. The jet was owned by David Pratt & partners when photographed on 19 December 1982.

As an end-of-tour treat the author scrounged a trip in this Westland Lynx XZ695 '400' disembarked from the Type 42 destroyer HMS *Glasgow*. Piloting the Lynx for the two-hour trip over the Straits of Gibraltar was Lt Peter Ritchings, with Sub Lt John Davies as his Observer.

This British Aerospace 146 ZD696 was one of a pair evaluated by the RAF's 241 Operational Conversion Unit and No.10 Sqdn at Brize Norton during 1983 for use with The Queen's Flight. '696 is shown here on a visit to Gibraltar. On completion of the trials the two 146s were returned to the manufacturer. Three fresh 146s were eventually bought for VIP use, the first of which was handed over to the Captain of the Queen's Flight in April 1986.

'Smoke on – Go!' The Red Arrows – all ten of them in this formation – arrive at Gibraltar in September 1986 prior to giving a display at the Station's Open Day. In the background can be seen two P-3 Orions (Dutch Navy and US Navy), plus two Alpha Jet trainers. (*Sean McCourt*).

Like generations of training aircraft before them, RAF Hawks began using Gibraltar as a destination for navigational exercises. Shown here are aircraft displaying the tiger head markings (on the fin) of No.74 (Reserve) Sqdn, part of 4 FTS, Valley, and wearing both black and grey paint schemes. (*RAF Gibraltar*).

The tone-down paint scheme on this Chinook cloaks it in anonymity so effectively that only its parent 'Royal Air Force' can be discerned. At least the location of the activity, involving an under-slung load which looks very like a bomb disposal robot, is apparent. (*RAF Gibraltar*).

Approaching to land from the west in April 1998 with La Linea's high-rise flats as a backdrop, this is no ordinary Hercules. It is actually an MC-130H Combat Talon II, probably from the USAF's 8th Special Operations Sqdn, Hulbert Field. The enlarged nose radome houses an Emerson Electric APQ-170 ground-mapping/weather/terrain-following radar. This system can 'look into the turn' to provide terrain-avoidance information as the aircraft manoeuvres through hilly or mountainous areas. (*Peter Green*).